D1540684

# I READ ABOUT GOD'S CARE

BY
Laura Alden

STANDARD PUBLISHING
Cincinnati, Ohio
2952

# Illustrators:

Gwen Connelly, Pages 8, 10, 11, 18, 26, 80-81, 94
Helen Endres, Pages 12-17, 19, 20, 75-77, 116-119
Diana Magnuson, Pages 22-25, 121-123
Pat Karch, Pages 27, 28, 60-63, 68-70, 105
Alicia Austin, Pages 30-36
James Seward, Pages 39-49
Lydia Halverson, Pages 50-53, 74, 78, 79, 97-99
Andre LeBlanc, Pages 55-59, 111, 113
Dan Siculan, Pages 65, 66, 114
Mina Gow McLean, Pages 72, 73, 106-109
Lois Axeman, Pages 82-87
Robert Masheris, Pages 90-93, 100-105

Cover Art by Nan Pollard

Unless otherwise noted, Scripture quotations are from
THE HOLY BIBLE: NEW INTERNATIONAL VERSION,
copyright © 1978 by the New York International Bible
Society. Used by permission.

Prepared for Standard Publishing by The Child's World.

ISBN 0-87239-662-2

I READ
ABOUT
GOD'S
CARE

# TABLE OF CONTENTS

## Stories

## Poems, Prayers, and Puzzles

# Bible Verses To Read

# Also in This Book

# Introduction

Have you ever asked yourself how a child today learns about God's care? The child has practically no contact with the Bible in the public school. Very little of his television viewing contains material of a Christian nature. So it is up to parents and Bible teachers to provide opportunities for the child to learn of God—to learn how God cares so much that He gave His only Son.

Every child should be taught to read Bible stories with pleasure and understanding. The Basic Bible Readers can help in this task.

*I Read About God's Care* is the third in the series of readers. It contains stories that were selected and written for the child who is in the second grade.

While the readers will be used mostly in the home, they also are valuable for Christian day schools and for the Bible school. And copies should be in every church library!

*Parents* may plan family devotions around some of the stories or poems. They also should encourage their children to read for themselves and should help with the decoding of Bible words.

*Sunday-school teachers* may include the readers on their browsing tables. They also will want to use them to supplement curriculum.

*Christian day schools* probably will wish to provide copies for each pupil.

A child will learn of God's care only if someone takes the time to provide opportunity. We should all be busy about that! And Basic Bible Readers will help us.

# Following A Tradition

The new Basic Bible Readers are a beautiful up-to-date edition of the famous Standard Bible Story Readers by Lillie A. Faris, that were first printed in 1925—and last revised in 1962. Millions of copies of these books have been added to the libraries of homes, schools, and churches.

The best of the former readers has been retained, including the favorite Bible stories that forever appeal to children. But the stories have been rewritten with a fresh, up-to-date approach. And all of the illustrations are new—drawn by noted children's artists of today.

Whether it's a beginning reader with his very own primer, an older child enjoying his developing reading skills, or a parent, teacher, or grandparent, we think all will heartily agree: some traditions are worth preserving!

# New Testament

### LONG, LONG AGO

Winds thru the olive trees
    Softly did blow
Round little Bethlehem
    Long, long ago.

Sheep on the hillside lay
    Whiter than snow,
Shepherds were watching them,
    Long, long ago.

Then from the happy sky,
    Angels bent low
Singing their songs of joy,
    Long, long ago.

For in a manger bed,
    Cradled we know,
Christ came to Bethlehem,
    Long, long ago.

—Anonymous

# A SPECIAL BABY

Joseph knocked on the door of the inn. Mary stood beside him.

The door opened a bit. "No room," said the innkeeper.

"Please," said Joseph. "We have come a long way."

"So have many others," said the innkeeper. Then he saw Mary. She was going to have a baby—any minute.

"There's a stable in back," said the innkeeper. "Go there."

Late in the night, the innkeeper heard a baby cry. The donkey in the stable heard him too. So did the oxen. And the lambs.

"His name is Jesus," Mary said softly.

"Yes," Joseph said.

Mary laid the baby in a manger filled with

straw. Then she sat beside Him.

As she looked at baby Jesus, she thought of all the things that had happened.

She thought of the angel who had come to her. "You will have a son," the angel had said. "He will be God's Son. You will call Him Jesus."

She thought of her husband, Joseph. An angel had told Joseph that the baby would be special—God's Son.

Shouts came from outside. Joseph jumped up. Mary reached for baby Jesus. The animals looked at the door.

In came shepherds. Old ones. Young ones. They came in quietly, one by one.

Looking at baby Jesus, the shepherds were filled with peace. They knelt to worship Him.

One very old shepherd knelt close by the manger. His eyes were full of tears.

Mary put Jesus back in the manger. The old shepherd's voice shook. "It is true," he whispered. "It is just as the angel said, 'A Savior is born!'. . . . The angel said He would be here, in

a manger. Glory to God! And on earth—
peace!"

And as the shepherds knelt before Jesus,
Mary felt peace, too. God would take care of
Joseph and her. And He would take care of His
Son.

# MORE THAN WOODEN PIECES

The nativity of Jesus
is more than just a scene.
It's more than wooden pieces
standing still and so serene.

The nativity of Jesus
is more than just a birth.
It's more than cries and swaddling clothes.
It brought new Life to earth.

The nativity of Jesus
is more than just one day.
For the Baby born that silent night
brings peace for every day.

# CHRIST IS CHRISTMAS

Who is glad that Jesus was born? Which pictures show things we can do to remember Jesus at Christmas?

## AT THE TEMPLE

Mary and Joseph were taking baby Jesus to Jerusalem. They were taking Him to God's house, the temple.

Mary bundled up baby Jesus. She wanted Him to stay wrapped-up warm. Joseph got everything ready for the trip.

Mary and Joseph walked and walked and walked. The trip took a long time. At last they came near to Jerusalem. They came to a hill from which they could see the city. And in the city, shining in the sunlight, was God's house, the temple. Mary and Joseph hurried into Jerusalem. They hurried into God's house.

In the temple was an old man named Simeon.

Simeon was a very special old man. He loved God. He tried hard to please God in all things.

God had made a promise to Simeon long ago. He had promised Simeon that he would live to see God's Son.

When Simeon saw baby Jesus, he said, "I have waited many years for this day." He took baby Jesus into his arms.

Simeon thanked God for letting him see Jesus. "I have seen Your Son as You promised," Simeon said. "He has come to be the Savior. Now I can die in peace."

Also in the temple that day was an old woman named Anna. She lived at the temple. She, too, loved God. She prayed to Him both day and night.

When she saw baby Jesus, Anna thanked God too. "He is the Savior," she said.

Mary and Joseph listened to Simeon and Anna. They wondered at the things they heard.

Mary and Joseph made an offering to God. Later, they took baby Jesus back to Bethlehem.

## THE WISE VISITORS

Far, far away from Bethlehem, some Wise-men saw a star. It was very big and very bright.

The Wise-men knew the star meant something special had happened. So they got on their camels to follow the star.

Day after day, the Wise-men traveled. They got tired. They got lonesome for home. But they

did not turn back. They kept following the star.

At last, the Wise-men came to Jerusalem. The star seemed to stop there. The Wise-men went to see the king in Jerusalem. His name was Herod.

"Where is the new King?" they asked. "We saw His star in the East. We want to worship Him."

King Herod did not know anything about a new King. So he asked his helpers. They said, "Look in Bethlehem."

"Go to Bethlehem," Herod told the Wise-men. "And let me know if you find this new king. I want to worship him too."

In Bethlehem, the Wise-men found Jesus. They were so glad to see Him!

They gave Jesus the gifts they had carried for such a long way. Gold. Frankincense. Myrrh. These were the best gifts the Wise-men could give. They were gifts fit for a king.

Now it was time for the Wise-men to start home. But they did not go back through Jerusalem. God told them not to tell Herod anything. Herod did not really want to worship Jesus. Herod wanted to kill Him.

So the Wise-men went home another way. But they were happy. They had seen the King!

"Then they opened their treasures
and presented him with gifts of gold
and of incense and of myrrh."

—Matthew 2:11

# LORD, TEACH ME

Lord, teach me all that I should know;
In grace and wisdom may I grow;
The more I learn to do Thy will,
The better may I love Thee still.

—Isaac Watts

## JESUS GROWS UP

Jesus lived in a house in the city of Nazareth. He lived with Mary and Joseph.

Mary and Joseph took good care of Jesus. And they taught Him many things.

Joseph was a carpenter. A carpenter is someone who makes things from wood. Jesus liked to help Joseph. Jesus helped Joseph build lots of things. Jesus learned to be a good carpenter.

Joseph taught God's Word to his family. He talked to his family about God. And about God's commands.

"You must love the Lord your God. You must love Him with all your heart," Joseph taught his family.

Jesus went to school with other children. The children learned to read and write. They learned about God and God's Word.

The teacher at the school loved God. He told many Bible stories to the students.

Sometimes Jesus played with other children. They played games like the ones you play. The Bible says that children in the market place played make-believe games. Sometimes they had running races. They had a good time.

Jesus grew and grew. He learned many things. And He remembered the things He learned.

God was pleased with Jesus. People were pleased with Jesus too.

*"Jesus grew in wisdom and stature, and in favor with God and men."*

—*Luke 2:52*

# JESUS AND JOHN

*"There came a man who was sent from God; his name was John."*
—John 1:6

People whispered about John the Baptist. They said he came out of the desert. He ate grasshoppers. He looked like a wild man. And he wore clothes made of camel's hair.

But people listened to what John said. For John the Baptist had a message from God. Day after day, he spoke to the people by the Jordan River.

"Are you sorry for your sins?" John asked. "Then you must change how you live. And you must change now! The Savior is coming!"

Many people believed John. They were sorry for their sins. And John baptized them in the Jordan.

Some people thought John was the Savior.

"I am not!" said John. "But I am here to tell you to get ready for Him."

And then, one day, Jesus came to the Jordan. John saw Him and knew that the Savior had come at last.

Jesus wanted to be baptized. But John did not think he should baptize the Son of God.

"I should be baptized by You!" John cried.

But Jesus said, "Baptize me." John's hands shook. He walked into the Jordan and baptized God's Son.

The sky opened up. A dove flew down and rested on Jesus. "You are my Son, whom I love," said a voice from heaven. "With You I am well pleased."

John knelt before Jesus. "I believe You *are* the Son of God," he whispered. "You have come at last."

# FOLLOW ME

Simon Peter and Andrew were washing their nets. "We've fished all night," said Peter. "And we haven't caught one little fish!"

"Shh," said Andrew. "There's Jesus. See Him? I'm trying to hear what He says."

Peter looked at the shore. A great crowd stood listening to Jesus. As Peter watched, the people moved closer and closer to Jesus. Jesus was almost in the water.

Still the people moved toward Jesus. Jesus stepped back into the water.

Jesus stepped back some more. And then, He stepped right into Peter's boat. Right into it!

"Can you put your boat out a little?" Jesus called to Peter.

Peter went to do as Jesus asked. He couldn't believe Jesus was in his boat!

Jesus spoke to the crowd from the boat.

At last, Jesus stopped talking. The people backed up and went away. "Go out deeper," Jesus said to Peter. "Then you can catch some fish."

"Lord, we fished all last night. There's nothing here."

Jesus just smiled at Peter.

"All right," Peter said after a minute. "All right, because You say so."

Peter put the boat out. Andrew put the nets down. And right away, the nets were filled with fish! The nets began to break!

"James! John!" Andrew called their friends to help.

Soon both boats were filled with fish. More fish than Peter and Andrew had ever seen!

Simon Peter fell on his knees before Jesus. "Go away from me, Lord!" he said. "I am a sinful man."

But Jesus said, "Do not be afraid. Follow me. I will teach you to fish for men."

The men could hardly wait to get to shore. When they did, they jumped out. And, leaving everything behind, they followed Him.

*"Come, follow me," Jesus said,*
*"and I will make you fishers of men."*

*—Matthew 4:19*

# A HOLE IN THE ROOF

Once there was a man who was very sick. His legs would not work. When he tried to stand up, he fell. The doctors could not make him well.

But the man had good friends. And one day they heard some good news. They ran to tell their sick friend.

"Jesus is in town," they said. "You must go see Him. He can make you well."

"But I can't go see Jesus," the sick man said. "I can't go anywhere."

That was true. His friends wondered what to do.

"I know!" said one friend. "We will take you to Jesus. You can lie on your bed."

The sick man wasn't sure this would work. But his friends thought it would. So he said yes. His friends picked up his bed.

It was easy to find Jesus. Many people stood around the house where He was. They stood around the door. They pushed and climbed and crawled to get inside.

The sick man and his friends could not get close to the door. How would they ever get in?

Then one friend saw the stairs on the outside of the house. He said, "Let's go up the stairs! Then we will be on the roof! Jesus will be right under us."

"Yes!" said another. "We can make a hole in the roof. We can put the bed down through the hole. Then Jesus will help us!"

The sick man wasn't sure this would work. But his friends thought it would. So he said yes.

His friends carried the bed up the stairs. They put it down on the flat roof. They tied ropes around it.

They dug through the roof. They made a big hole.

They picked up the bed. They held onto the ropes. Down, down, down through the hole went the bed with their sick friend.

The bed went down through the hole right to the place where Jesus was.

Jesus looked at the man who could not walk. Jesus looked at the men who had brought their friend to Him. He smiled up at them.

Then Jesus said to the sick man, "Stand up, pick up your bed, and go home."

Suddenly, the sick man was not sick anymore. He got up. He picked up his bed. He went home.

Everyone saw what Jesus did. They looked at Him. They looked back at the man. "We have never seen anything like this!" they said.

# THE MAN WHO COULD NOT SEE

"Help me!
Please help me!"

It was the blind man calling for help. He often called for help.

The man had never seen anything. He had never seen his mother. He had never seen his father. He had never seen the sunshine. He had never seen a flower.

He was blind as a baby. He was blind as a boy. He grew up to be a man, and he was still blind.

One day Jesus was in the city where the blind man lived.

"Help me. Please help me. I cannot see!" said the blind man.

Jesus looked at the blind man. He loved him. He knew God loved him too. And Jesus wanted His followers to know that God cared.

So Jesus walked over to the man. He spat on the ground. He made some mud.

Jesus put the mud on the eyes of the blind man. Then He said, "Go wash in the pool of Siloam."

The blind man did what Jesus said. And then . . . he could see! He saw the pool. He saw the sunshine. He saw people all around him. The blind man wasn't blind anymore!

The man's neighbors and others who knew him wondered. "Isn't this the blind man?" they asked.

"Yes, I am he," the man said. "Once I was blind. But now, because of Jesus, I see."

# THE ONE WHO CAME BACK

"Jesus! Master!"

From far away, Jesus heard voices calling. Looking, He saw eight . . . nine . . . ten men. He saw that the men were sick with leprosy. Bad sores were all over their bodies.

Jesus knew why the men did not come close to Him. Lepers could not get close to anyone. Leprosy was a very bad sickness. No one wanted to catch leprosy.

"Help us!" the lepers called. They had heard about Jesus. They believed He could make them well.

The sick men came as close to Jesus as they dared. "Help us, Jesus! Please help us!"

Jesus felt sorry for the men. So He said to them, "Go and see the priests."

Jesus said this because He was going to heal the men. But He knew that a priest must also say that they were well. Only then could they live in town with everyone else.

The ten men turned to go. They would do what Jesus said.

The men walked away. They didn't feel any different . . . or did they? Something was happening!

The lepers looked at themselves. They looked at each other. Then they began running. They ran toward town, shouting and laughing. They were well. They were *well!*

Suddenly, one man stopped. He turned

around. He ran back to Jesus.

"Master, You have made me well!" the man said. "Thank You! Praise God!"

Jesus looked around. "Were there not ten?" He asked. "Where are the other nine?"

Jesus was sad that nine of the ten did not come back to say, "Thank You." But He was glad for the one.

Jesus said, "Get up. Go your way. Because you believed in me, you are well."

# GOD CARES

Jesus wanted to show people that God cared about them. So God gave Jesus the power to make people well.

Remember?

Did Jesus tell these men they would be better in a few days? Or did Jesus tell them He could not help them? Or did Jesus use God's power to make the men well right away?

## THE BIG STORM

There is a pretty lake in the land where Jesus lived. It is called Galilee. Jesus and His helpers often sailed on the lake.

One day, Jesus had been very busy. He had made many sick people well. He was very tired.

"Let's go across the lake," Jesus said.

Jesus and His friends got into a boat. They started across Galilee. Jesus fell asleep.

In a little while, a storm came up. The wind began to blow. Dark clouds made the sky black and scary.

The wind blew harder. Waves rocked the boat.

The waves got higher still. And then water came over the sides of the boat.

Jesus' friends were afraid. They knew the boat was not safe in such a big storm. They did not think they could get to the other side of the lake. Maybe they would drown.

"Wake Jesus!" someone shouted. "He can help us!"

"Teacher!" they shouted. "Teacher, don't You care if our boat sinks? We all are going to drown!"

Jesus woke up. He saw that His friends were afraid.

Jesus stood up in the boat. He talked to the wind and the sea. He said, "Quiet! Be still!"

The wind stopped blowing. The waves went away. Galilee got very quiet.

Jesus' friends were quiet, too. They had never seen anything like this.

"What kind of man is this?" they asked each other. "Even the wind and waves obey Him."

Their boat came to the other side of Galilee. Jesus and His friends got out—safe and sound.

Jesus' friends were filled with wonder. They now thought that Jesus could do anything in the world.

He could make sick people well. He could make blind people see. He could even make the wind obey Him!

*"Are not two sparrows sold for a penny? Yet not one of them will fall to the ground apart from the will of your Father. . . . So don't be afraid; you are worth more than many sparrows."*

—Matthew 10:29, 31

# ON A ROCKY ROAD

Robbers were hiding beside the road.

One robber said, "When someone comes along, jump on him. Take his money. Then run away fast."

"Take everything," another robber said.

A man came down the road. He was on his way to Jericho.

Seeing him, the robbers jumped out from behind a big rock.

They hit the man. They beat him up. They took his money. They took his coat. They took everything. Then they ran away.

The man lay by the side of the road. His head hurt. His legs hurt. He hurt all over. He could not even get up.

Then he heard footsteps.

A man was coming down the road. A man who worked in God's house. He would stop and help!

But he didn't! He looked at the hurt man. Then he crossed the road. And kept walking!

The hurt man almost cried. He needed help right away! Then he heard more footsteps.

Another man came down the road. This man worked in God's house too. Surely he would help.

But he didn't! He just looked at the hurt man. Then he turned and walked away.

The hurt man was alone. Would he die by
the side of the road?

For a long time, the hurt man heard nothing. Then, "clip-clop, clip-clop, clip-clop, clip-clop." There was a man on a donkey.

The hurt man was so glad to know someone else was coming. But then he saw that the man was a Samaritan. His people were not friends with Samaritans. A Samaritan would never help him.

But then he heard a soft voice.

"You are hurt, my friend. Let me help you."

The Samaritan washed the hurt man's cuts and scratches. He put soft cloths on them. He put the hurt man on his donkey and took him to an inn.

"Here is some money," he told the inn-keeper. "Take care of this man. If you need more money, I will pay you when I come back."

The Samaritan got on his donkey and left. The hurt man stayed and got well.

Jesus told this story. At the end of it, He said, "Which man was a better friend to the man who was hurt?"

"The Samaritan," everyone said.

"Yes," Jesus said. He wanted people to learn to help others.

# JESUS AND THE CHILDREN

"Come on!" the children called. They raced to the road. Jesus was coming!

"Wait for us!" called their mothers, laughing.

Everyone was happy. Jesus made them happy.

The people shouted. There He was!

The children stood on their toes. But there were too many people. They couldn't see Jesus!

The children started to cry. How could they see Jesus?

"This way," said their mothers. They led the children closer to Jesus. "See Him now?"

"What do you think you're doing?" said a loud voice. It was one of Jesus' helpers.

The mothers stopped. The children stopped.

"We want our children to see Jesus," said a mother.

"We're going to see Jesus," said a little boy.

"Jesus is very busy," said the man. "He is too busy to see the children."

Jesus stood up. He had heard His helper.

"Let the little children come to me," He said.

The children ran to Jesus. They sat down beside Him. He smiled at them. They smiled back. Jesus and the children had a good time together.

For Jesus loves little children—and big children, too.

# I LOVE JESUS

Jesus loves children. Do you love Him?

You can love Jesus wherever you are—at home, at school, at church, or at play.

Find the pictures that go with these places:

AT HOME
AT SCHOOL
AT CHURCH
AT PLAY

*"Zacchaeus . . . being a short man . . . climbed a . . . tree to see . . . Jesus."* —Luke 19:2-4

# THE MAN IN THE TREE

Zacchaeus shut his eyes. The sun was hot. He was hot. And there were people all around him. People in front of him. People behind him.

Zacchaeus opened his eyes. He wanted so much to see Jesus. But he could not see above the people. He was too short to see a thing. All these people!

Suddenly Zacchaeus had an idea. He knew which way Jesus would be walking. Zacchaeus worked his way out of the crowd. He ran down the road. He came to a large sycamore tree.

Zacchaeus climbed up into the tree. He climbed . . . higher and higher.

"Now," he said. "Now I can see everything." Zacchaeus sat way up in the tree.

He looked down. He saw Jesus coming!

Zacchaeus watched Jesus. He saw Jesus stop and talk to people. "Maybe He will talk to me," thought Zacchaeus.

Jesus came closer. He walked under the tree. He stopped. He looked up at Zacchaeus.

"Zaccheus, come down!" Jesus said, smiling. "I will stay at your house today."

Zaccheus almost fell out of the tree. Jesus would come to his house! How happy he was!

Some people were not so happy. They did not like Zacchaeus. "He is a bad man," they said to each other. "Jesus should not go home with such a bad man."

But Jesus went home with Zacchaeus. Jesus knew Zacchaeus could change.

And Zacchaeus wanted to change. He knew he had not been good. His job was to make people pay money to the king. Sometimes he made them pay too much. Then he kept some of the money.

Zacchaeus was very sorry.

"Lord," Zacchaeus said. "I will give half of my money to the poor people. And I will give money to the people I cheated. I'll give them four times as much as I took from them!"

Jesus was glad. He said, "Now you belong to me. I came to save people like you, Zacchaeus."

Zacchaeus was happy. He knew he would never be the same. He had changed. He had met Jesus.

# MARY, MARTHA, AND LAZARUS

Martha hurried to fix dinner for Jesus. She wanted to make good food for Him. But she would need some help. Where was that Mary?

Martha looked for her sister. She wanted her help—now! Then she saw Mary, talking with Jesus!

"Mary," Martha whispered. "Mary!"

Mary did not look up. She did not hear Martha.

Martha walked over to Jesus. "Jesus," said Martha. "Tell my sister to help!"

"Martha, Martha," Jesus said. "You make such good food for me. But it is better, sometimes, to listen. Mary knows that."

Later, Martha thought about what Jesus said. She would remember. And she would take time to listen to Jesus.

*** 

Jesus loved Mary and Martha. He loved their brother, Lazarus, too.

One day, Lazarus got very sick. Mary and Martha were afraid he would die. They asked Jesus to come. Then they waited.

Lazarus got sicker and sicker. Still, Mary and Martha waited for Jesus. He did not come. Lazarus died.

Mary and Martha were very sad. They would miss their brother.

Then Jesus came.

"My brother would not have died if You had been here," Martha said.

Mary fell at Jesus' feet, crying.

Jesus cried too. He loved Mary and Martha. He loved Lazarus.

Jesus went to the tomb. "Take away the stone," He said. Then He stretched out His arms. He called, "Lazarus, come out!"

And Lazarus came out of the tomb! Alive! People saw him walk. They heard him talk.

And many believed in Jesus.

# THE SPARROW AND THE ROBIN

*Said the sparrow to the robin, "I*
*should really like to know*
*Why these anxious human beings*
*rush about and worry so."*
*Said the robin to the sparrow, "I*
*think that it must be*
*That they have no Heavenly Father*
*such as cares for you and me."*

—Elizabeth Cheney

## JESUS SAYS GOOD-BY

Jesus always told people about God, His Father. And He told them about Heaven.

Jesus wanted people to know how beautiful it is in Heaven. Jesus knew that He would be going to Heaven soon. His work on earth was almost done.

Jesus knew that His friends could not go with Him. But He wanted them to know that some day they could be with Him again—in Heaven.

Jesus' friends were sad when He told them He was going away. They did not know what they would do without Him.

Jesus told them not to be sad or afraid. Here is what Jesus said. These are His own words:

Let not your heart be troubled:
ye believe in God, believe also in me.
In my Father's house are many mansions:
if it were not so,
I would have told you.
I go to prepare a place for you.
And if I go and prepare a place for you,
I will come again,
and receive you unto myself;
that where I am,
there ye may be also.
—John 14:1-3 KJV

Jesus' friends felt better. They believed what
Jesus said. They knew He loved them. And they
would try to live His way—no matter what.

## JESUS GOES HOME

There were people who did not like Jesus. They did not believe He was God's Son, the Savior. They did not want Him around. They wanted Him dead! Finally, they had their way. Jesus was put to death on a cross!

His enemies were happy now. But His friends were very, very sad. They loved Jesus. They did not know how they could live without Him. Some of Jesus' friends took His body and put it into a tomb. Others watched. Then, slowly and sadly, His friends went away. They thought they would never see Jesus again.

But Jesus had told them that He would not stay dead. And He didn't!

\*\*\*

Three days after Jesus died, some of Jesus' friends came to His tomb. They found that Jesus'

body was not there. Two angels were in the tomb.

"Jesus is not here," said one angel. "He has risen! Go quickly and tell His helpers."

Jesus' helpers could hardly believe the news! But later that day, they knew it was true. For Jesus, himself, appeared to them.

***

During the next forty days, Jesus visited His helpers many times. Others saw Jesus too. Once He visited more than 500 people at one time. During this time, Jesus said to His helpers, "Wait in Jerusalem until you receive power from God. Then tell others about me. Tell people here and all over the world."

Then one day Jesus met His helpers on a hill just outside Jerusalem. As He talked with them, suddenly He began to rise up into the air. Finally a cloud hid Him from their sight.

As His helpers watched, two angels stood beside them. The angels said, "Why do you stand looking into the sky? Jesus will come again in the same way that you saw Him go."

Jesus' helpers hurried to do as Jesus had asked. They knew that Jesus had gone to be with

God. And they knew that someday, He would return—just as the angels had said.

# THE DAY THE CHURCH BEGAN

It was Pentecost—a special holiday. Jesus' helpers were together in Jerusalem. Jesus had told them to wait there. He had said, "You will receive power from God."

Suddenly the power came. The disciples heard a sound from Heaven—like a mighty wind! The sound filled the house!

Suddenly flames of fire sat over each of them.

And right away, they were filled with God's Spirit. They began to speak in languages they didn't know!

Jews from many countries were in Jerusalem for the holiday. Hearing the noise, crowds of them came running to see what it was all about. They were stunned to hear their own languages spoken by Jesus' helpers.

After some time, one helper, Peter, stood up to preach to the crowd. He told them about Jesus. He told them that Jesus was God's Son, the Savior. He said, "You have killed Jesus!"

When Peter finished preaching, the people said, "What should we do?"

Peter replied, "Turn from your sin. Be baptized."

Before the day was over, more than 3000 people believed in Jesus and were baptized.

The church had begun.

*"Sing to the Lord a new song; sing to the Lord, all the earth. Sing to the Lord, praise his name; proclaim his salvation day after day."*

—Psalm 96:1, 2

*"It is good to praise the Lord and make music to your name, O Most High, to proclaim your love in the morning and your faithfulness at night."*

—*Psalm 92:1, 2*

# THE COMING OF THE KING

by Laura E. Richards

One day, some children in another land were on a playground. Suddenly a man ran past, shouting, "The king! The king will come this way today. Get ready for the king!"

The children stopped playing. "Did you hear that?" one asked.

"The king is coming," said another. "What if he stops here?"

The children looked around. Broken toys and bits of paper lay all around.

"We'd better clean this place up," said one little boy.

So they did. It was hard work. It took a long time. But when they were done, the playground was beautiful.

The children waited all day for the king. They waited and waited. But the king did not come. But just before the sun went down, an old man with worn-out clothes and a kind, tired face passed by.

He stopped to look through the fence. "What a pretty place," the old man said. "May I come in and rest?"

"Oh, yes," the children said. They brought him in and helped him to a seat.

"This is our playground," one girl said. "We cleaned it up because we thought the king was coming this way. He never came. But we are going to keep it like this anyway."

The old man was very tired. He sat and rested. The children wanted to make him feel better. So they told him their best secrets.

They told him about the puppies in the

barn, about the tree with the bird's nest, and about the seashore with the shells.

After a while, the man asked for a cup of cold water. The children brought it to him in their best cup.

Then the old man thanked the children and got up to go.

The children waved to him as he went slowly down the road. By then, the sun was setting.

"He looked so tired," said one of them.

"But he was so nice," said another.

"Yes," said still another. "The king didn't come. But I'm glad we could let the old man rest here. I'm glad he stopped to talk with us!"

\*\*\*

The children in the story were kind to the old man. They were as kind as they would have been to the king.

Jesus told *us* to be kind. He wants us to be as kind to others as we would be to Him.

"The Coming of the King" from *The Golden Wings* by Laura Lee Richards. © 1903 Little, Brown & Co.

# Old Testament

# GOD MADE THE WORLD

*"In the beginning God
created the heavens
and the earth."*—Genesis 1:1

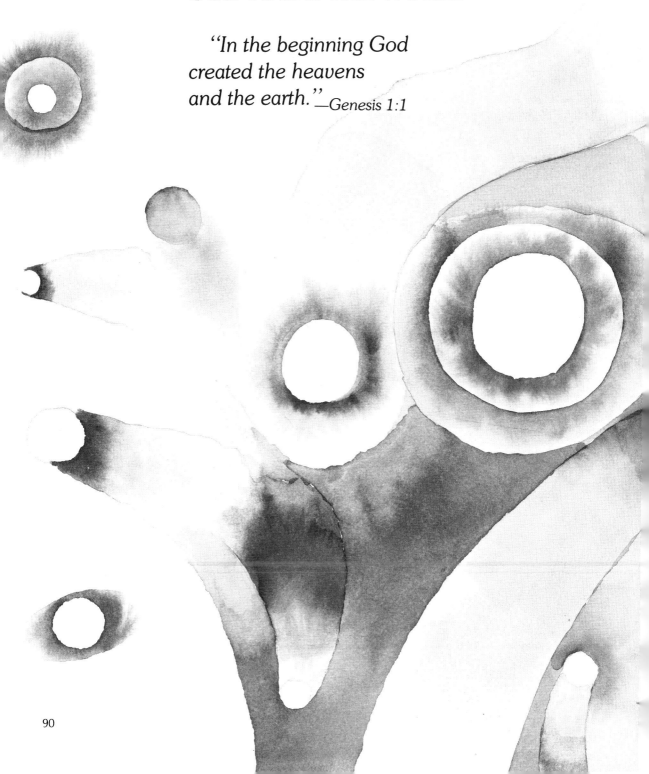

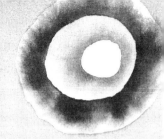

Once there was no world. There was only God.

Then God made the heavens and the earth. But everything was very dark.

So God said, "Let there be light." And there was light. God called the light day. He called the darkness night.

Next God made the sky. Then God put water into seas. And He let dry land appear.

And God saw that it was good.

On the land God made grass. He made seeds to grow flowers and food. He made trees and all the plants that grow.

God made the sun to give us light and keep us warm. He made the moon and stars to shine at night.

And God saw that it was good.

Then God made birds. He gave them wings and pretty colors. God made all the birds that fly in the sky. Then he made fish and whales and all the things that swim.

And God saw that it was good.

Next, God made animals. He made some animals to climb trees. He made some to run fast. He made others to live underground.

God saw that it was all good.

Then God made people. He made a man and a woman. The man's name was Adam. The woman's name was Eve.

Adam and Eve lived in a garden called Eden. They saw all the wonderful things God made.

Adam and Eve took care of the garden for God.

And it was very good.

# GOD MADE THE ANIMALS

God made animals of all kinds. There are ten different animals in the picture below. See if you can find them all—bear, deer, elephant, giraffe, lion, monkey, rabbit, parrot, pig, zebra.

## THE CREATION

*All things bright and beautiful,*
  *All creatures great and small,*
*All things wise and wonderful,*
  *The Lord God made them all.*

—Cecil Frances Alexander

# THE GREAT LADDER

"How tired I am!" Jacob said. "I must find a place to rest."

Jacob walked slowly. He *was* tired—and sad, too. He had just left his home. He had just left his father and mother. He had just left his brother.

Jacob would miss his father and mother. But he would not miss his brother. Jacob had had a big fight with his brother. That was why he was running away.

"Here," said Jacob. "Here's a place to stop."

He lay down and put his head on a stone. Now it was dark. Stars shone in the sky.

Jacob looked up at the stars. "What will happen to me now?" he wondered. Soon he fell asleep.

And then Jacob had a dream. He saw a ladder—a very long ladder. It reached from earth to Heaven.

Jacob saw angels on the ladder. Some angels were going up the ladder. Some angels

were coming down. God spoke to Jacob from the top of that long ladder.

"I am the Lord, Jacob. I am the God of your father. I will give you and your children the land where you are sleeping. I will give you more land than you can see!

"I am with you, Jacob. You will have many children. Good things will happen to you and to them. I will keep you safe wherever you go. And I will bring you back to this land."*

When Jacob woke up, he said, "God was here! This must be the house of God! I have seen the gate to Heaven."

Jacob set a stone up on its end.

"I will mark this place," he said. "I will call it, 'The House of God.' "

Then Jacob left the land. He stayed away for many years.

* paraphrased from
   Genesis 28:13-15.

But one day Jacob came back, just as God had said he would.

God had kept Jacob safe. God had given him many children. And He had given him the land He had promised.

God always keeps His promises!

## HEBREW BABY

"Shh, Baby, don't cry!" whispered Miriam. She heard someone coming. She hid behind the bulrushes.

Rock, rock. The Nile River rocked the baby in the basket. He stopped crying.

Just in time, too. Miriam peeped from her hiding place. She saw a group of people. . . . Who were they? . . . Then, Miriam was afraid! The king's daughter and her helpers were coming!

The king ruled Egypt. And he had said that all Hebrew boy babies were to be killed. That was why Miriam's mother had hid her baby. That was why he lay in the basket now—to fool the king, to stay alive.

But now the king's daughter would find him! Miriam didn't know what to do. So she just waited—and prayed for her baby brother.

The princess saw the basket. She pointed to it. "Let's see what's in it," she said.

A servant took the basket to the king's daughter.

Miriam watched carefully.

The princess opened the basket. The baby was crying. "Poor baby!" she said. "You must be one of the Hebrew babies my father ordered killed. I won't let you be killed. I'll take you to be my own child."

Now! Miriam thought. She crawled out of the bulrushes. She ran to the king's daughter.

"Shall I get a Hebrew mother to take care of the baby for you?" Miriam asked.

"Yes, go."

Miriam ran to get her mother.

Miriam's mother shut her eyes. "God has saved him," she said. Tears ran down her cheeks.

"Come, Mother," Miriam said. "The princess is waiting."

They ran all the way. The princess put the baby in his mother's arms. "Take care of him for me," she said.

The mother took the baby into her arms. She held him close. How happy she was! Her baby was safe!

Later, he would go to live in the palace. He would be named Moses. And he would do a special work for God.

# GOD SENDS FOOD

Moses' people were slaves in Egypt. The king made them work very hard. He was very mean to them. So they cried out to God for help.

God heard their cries. He promised them a land all their own. It was a land far away from Egypt, far away from the bad king.

God told Moses to take the people there.

So Moses went to the king. "Let my people go!" Moses said.

At first the king would not let the people go. But God was with Moses. The king could not win against God. So, at last, he let the people go.

Free! God's people headed for the land God had promised them. They talked about what it would be like. "A land flowing with milk and honey," God had said.

That meant the people would be able to get food from the land. It would be a good place to live.

But to get there, the people had to walk through the desert. It was a long trip. And the people ran out of food.

"We are going to die!" the people cried. "Even in Egypt, we had food!"

Again God heard the cries of His people. He did not want them to die. So He sent them food. He sent quail each evening. Each morning He sent food from the sky. Manna.

The people shouted and cried for joy. They ran to pick up the manna. They put it in jars. They baked it into bread. They ate manna and more manna.

Each day—except on Saturday, the Sabbath (a day of rest and worship for the Jews)—the manna fell. On Friday everyone would pick up enough for two days. There was always enough. God took good care of His people.

# THE FALL OF JERICHO

After many years, God's people came to the promised land. They were glad to stop walking. They were happy to be in their new land.

But the people who lived in the land were not so happy. They did not want any new people.

Their cities had high walls. How could God's people ever get inside one?

"Do not be afraid," God told the people. "I will give you this land."

The people knew that God would take care of them. He had brought them out of Egypt. He had given them food. And He would give them this land.

God told Joshua how to get into a city named Jericho.

Each day the people were to march around the walls of Jericho. First their soldiers would march. Then seven men with trumpets would follow.

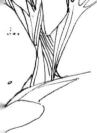

Then all of the people would join the march. No one would talk or even whisper. The people were all to be very quiet.

This is what they were to do each day for six days.

On the seventh day, they were to march around the city seven times. The seven men would blow their trumpets.

Then the people would shout with a great shout. And the walls of the city would fall down!

The people wondered how God would do this. But God always did what He said He would do.

So the people got everything ready.

The first day they marched once around the walls of Jericho. The soldiers marched first. The seven men with trumpets marched behind them. Then all the people joined the march. They did not make any noise.

The next day every one marched again.
They did this each day for six days.

On the seventh day, the people marched
around the city seven times. The seven men
blew their trumpets.

Then the people shouted with a great shout.
And the walls of Jericho fell down!

God's people went into Jericho. God had
given it to them.

# DAVID AND THE GIANT

Once there was a shepherd boy named David.

One day David's father said, "I want you to go see your brothers. I want to send them some food."

David's brothers were soldiers. They had been gone a long time.

David was glad he would see his brothers. He took the food. He went a long way. At last, he found his brothers. "Why have you stayed so long?" David asked.

His brothers said, "The soldiers on the other side of the valley want to take the land away from us. But we are afraid to fight them because of their giant. His name is Goliath."

Just then the giant walked down into the valley.

David looked at him. He was very big.

"Run!" said David's brothers. "It's Goliath!"

Goliath laughed. "Send someone to fight me!" he yelled.

No one came.

Goliath laughed again. "Are you afraid? Will no one fight with me?"

David said, "Who is this that we should be afraid of him when God is helping us?"

Some of the king's soldiers heard David. One of them told King Saul what David said. Saul sent for David.

"I will fight the giant," David said.

"You are just a boy," the king said. "I cannot let you fight a giant."

"When I was watching my sheep," David said, "a lion came and got a lamb. I ran after the lion and killed it. Another time a bear came. I killed the bear too.

"God took care of me when the lion and the bear came. God will take care of me when I fight the giant."

"Go and the Lord be with you," Saul said.

David picked up five small stones. He took his slingshot and walked toward the giant.

Goliath saw him coming.

"What are you going to fight me with?" he roared. "Are you going to kill me with sticks?"

"You come with a sword and a spear," David said. "But God is with me."

Then David put one of the stones in his slingshot. He began to swing it. Around and around.

Faster and faster! Around and around!
There went the stone!

The stone hit Goliath in the head. And the
giant fell down, dead.

The king's soldiers clapped and shouted!
And they chased the soldiers of Goliath away.

## FLOUR FOR A WIDOW

"May I have a drink of water, please?" Elijah asked a widow.

God had told him to ask her for help.

"And a piece of bread?" Elijah asked.

The widow looked at Elijah. "I don't have any bread," she said, sadly. "I have only a handful of flour left. And a little bit of oil."

She picked up a stick. "I am going home now to start the fire. I will bake the last bit of bread for my boy and me. Then, we will go hungry until we die."

Elijah said, "Do not be afraid. Make some bread for me. You will have enough for you and your boy. God will give you enough."

The widow believed Elijah. And she trusted in God. She used her flour and oil to bake bread for Elijah.

After the widow was done baking, she went to put away her flour jar. She picked it up. It was not empty! She looked in her oil jug. It was not empty either!

God had given her flour and oil. And each day, there was always more. As long as she needed the flour and oil, there was always enough.

God took care of the widow, for the widow had believed Elijah. She had trusted in God.

# SERVANT GIRL

"God, watch over us this day," prayed the servant girl in the house of Naaman. She looked out the window toward Israel, her home. Then she went to see her mistress.

"Mistress?" said the girl.

Something was wrong. The wife of Naaman sat looking out of the window. There were tears on her face.

"Mistress?"

"Oh, child. . . . You can do my hair . . ."

What could be wrong? The little girl had never seen her mistress cry.

She picked up the combs. Her mistress sat very still.

And then, in a small voice, her mistress said, "Naaman is a leper. He is going to die."

Leper! The girl knew what that meant. Lepers had a very bad sickness. Their skin rotted away. And they always died.

The little girl wanted to cry. She liked Naaman. She liked Naaman's wife. The servant girl was sad all day.

That night, she prayed for Naaman. "God watch over us this night. And, please, God, please make my master well."

The next day, the little servant girl got up. She got dressed. She said her prayers. And then, she had an idea.

It was about Naaman. And about a man named Elisha.

Before Naaman's soldiers took her away, the little girl had lived in Israel. She had learned about God there. And she had learned about Elisha.

Elisha was God's prophet in Israel. Through him, God did many great things. Elisha could help make Naaman well.

The servant girl ran to her mistress. "Mistress!" she said. "If only my master could see the prophet Elisha! He could make my master well!"

"Elisha?"

"He is God's prophet in Israel," came the answer.

"Pray, then," said the wife of Naaman. "Pray to your God. I will tell Naaman about Elisha."

How happy Naaman was! He went to Israel. He went to see Elisha.

"Wash seven times in the Jordan River," said Elisha. "Do this and you will be well."

At first Naaman thought this would be silly. Why should he dip in the river seven times? How could that help?

But he went to the Jordan. He got into the water. He dipped once—nothing happened. He dipped a second time—nothing happened. He dipped a third . . . fourth . . . fifth . . . sixth time. . . .

And then he dipped the seventh time. And Naaman was well!

Because Naaman obeyed God's word as told to him by Elisha, he was made well!

Naaman thanked God. He thanked Elisha. And when he got home, he must surely have thanked his little servant.

# DANIEL AND THE LIONS

In a land far from Israel lived a king named Darius. He was a good king. But he did not believe in God.

In the same land lived a man named Daniel. Soldiers had taken Daniel from his home in Israel many years before. Daniel worked for King Darius.

But Daniel had not forgotten Israel. And he had not forgotten God. He prayed to Him three times a day.

King Darius liked Daniel. He made Daniel a ruler. Daniel worked hard for the king.

But some of the king's helpers did not like Daniel. These men were jealous of him. The king had Daniel do things they wanted to do. So the men thought of a way to kill Daniel.

They went to the king. "O king!" they said. "How great you are! All people should pray to you and only you."

The king was happy that his helpers liked him so much.

"O king," the men said. "Make a new law.
Make a law that people must pray only to you."

King Darius listened closely.

"And if anyone prays another way, he will
be put into the lions' den."

The king liked their idea. So he made the new law.

Daniel heard about the new law. He was sad. For Daniel could not pray to the king. Daniel prayed to God. And God only.

The king's men knew this. That is why they had the king make the law. So they watched Daniel. They saw him pray to God in the morning. They saw him pray at noon. They saw him pray at night.

They went and told the king.

The king was very sad. He did not want to put Daniel in the lions' den. But the king had made the law. And the king must keep the law.

Daniel was thrown into the lions' den.

"May your God keep you safe!" shouted King Darius to Daniel. "May your God let you live."

The king could not eat. He could not sleep. He did not want Daniel to die.

In the morning, Darius ran to the lions' den. Would Daniel still be alive?

"Daniel!" the king called. . . . "Daniel?"

"O king, live forever!" Daniel called back. "My God sent His angel. He shut the lions' mouths. They did not hurt me."

"Now your God will be my God!" said the king. "And all of my people will worship Him."

## New Basic Bible Vocabulary

Of the words used in *I Read About God's Care*, 653 are words included on the *EDL Vocabulary List* or the *Macmillan Basic Vocabulary List* of second grade (or below) words. Of the remaining words, 80 are repeated from the Cumulative Basic Bible Vocabulary listed in the Basic Bible Reader, Grade One, *I Read About God's Love*.

There are 108 new words necessary to the stories in this book. They are listed below.

13. oxen
14. knelt
15. knelt
19. bundled
    wrapped
20. Simeon
21. Anna
    offering
    Simeon
23. lonesome
    worship
24. worship
27. carpenter
28. commands
    heart
31. baptize
    baptized
    desert
    John the Baptist
    Jordan
    sins
    wore
32. baptize
    baptized
    dove
    John
    Jordan
    knelt
    whom

33. Simon Peter
34. Peter
35. James
    John
    Peter
36. Simon Peter
    sinful
43. sunshine
45. Siloam
    spat
    sunshine
46. dared
    lepers
    leprosy
    Master
    sickness
47. lepers
    Master
49. power
50. Galilee
52. Galilee
53. Galilee
55. Jericho
58. clip-clop
    Samaritan
59. Samaritan
    scratches
61. you're
63. church

64. sycamore
    Zacchaeus
65. Zacchaeus
66. Zacchaeus
67. cheated
    Zacchaeus
68. Martha
    Lazarus
69. Lazarus
    Martha
70. alive
    Lazarus
    Martha
    stretched
    tomb
72. Heaven
76. appeared
    death
    finally
    power
    rise
    risen
    Savior
    tomb
78. flames
    holiday
    Pentecost
    Peter
    power

preach
Spirit
stunned
79. baptized
    begun
    church
    Peter
    preaching
    replied
    sin
82. playground
83. playground
84. seashore
86. setting
91. appear
    heavens
93. Adam
    Eden
    Eve
94. giraffe
96. Heaven
    Jacob
    shone
97. Jacob
98. Heaven
    Jacob
99. Jacob
100. bulrushes
    Hebrew

|  |  |  |  |
|---|---|---|---|
| Miriam | Joshua | jug | master |
| Nile | seventh | trusted | mistress |
| 101. alive | trumpets | widow | Naaman |
| Hebrew | 108. Jericho | 116. Israel | prophet |
| group | trumpets | mistress | servant |
| Miriam | 109. Jericho | Naaman | 119. dip |
| servant | seventh | servant | dipped |
| 102. cheeks | trumpets | 117. leper | Elisha |
| Miriam | 110. Goliath | master | fifth |
| 103. slaves | 111. Goliath | mistress | Jordan |
| 104. desert | Saul | Naaman | Naaman |
| flowing | 112. slingshot | rotted | obeyed |
| 105. Jews | spear | servant | servant |
| manna | sword | sickness | seventh |
| quail | 113. Goliath | skin | sixth |
| Sabbath | 114. Elijah | 118. Elisha | 120. Israel |
| worship | widow | Israel | 122. alive |
| 107. Jericho | 115. Elijah | Jordan | thrown |
|  |  |  | 123. worship |

## Cumulative Basic Bible Vocabulary

The following list includes all the words introduced as new Bible words or words necessary to tell the Bible stories in the Basic Bible Primer and Basic Bible Readers, Grades One and Two.

| | | | |
|---|---|---|---|
| Adam | appear | begged | bother |
| afraid | appeared | begun | bought |
| against | area | believe | branches |
| alive | arms | below | bread |
| Amen | asleep | Bethlehem | break |
| among | Baa | Bible | bright |
| Andrew | babies | blanket | brighter |
| angels | baptize | bless | brightly |
| angry | baptized | blessed | broke |
| Anna | bath | blind | brought |
| answered | became | body | build |
| anyone | become | born | built |

bulrushes
bundled
busy
camels
careful
carpenter
carried
chance
chased
cheated
cheeks
cheerfully
Christmas
church
clear
clip-clop
comfort
commands
cost
counted
counts
cover
crippled
crowd
Daniel
dared
Darius
darkness
daughter
David
dead
deaf
death
den
desert
die
died
dip
dipped

done
donkey
dove
dream
dry
dying
earth
Eden
Egypt
Eli
Elijah
Elisha
enough
Eve
faint
fed
few
fields
fifth
finally
finished
flames
floated
flood
flowing
follow
followed
food
forty
frankincense
front
full
Galilee
gathered
gently
gifts
giraffe
God
goes

Goliath
goodness
grabbed
group
Hannah
happen
happened
hardly
harp
hate
hated
hay
healed
healthy
heart
Heaven
Hebrew
held
helpers
Herod
hillside
hit
holiday
holy
hope
hosanna
hugged
hundred
hungry
husband
idea
important
inn
innkeeper
Israel
Jacob
Jairus
James
jealous

Jericho
Jerusalem
Jesus
Jews
John
John the Baptist
Jordan
Joseph
Joshua
jug
kept
kill
killed
kindness
knelt
knew
laid
land
large
late
later
law
Lazarus
leader
learn
learned
led
left
leper
leprosy
lid
listened
listening
loaves
lonesome
Lord
loving
maid
manger

manna
market
Martha
Mary
master
meant
meet
messages
Miriam
mistress
months
moon
Moses
mouths
music
myrrh
Naaman
Nazareth
nearby
Nile
Noah
Nobleman
none
nurse
obey
obeyed
obeying
offering
often
ordered
own
owners
oxen
palace
palm
parents

passed
past
pay
Pentecost
perfect
Peter
Philip
pieces
playground
poor
poured
power
praised
praises
pray
prayed
praying
preach
preaching
presents
priest
princess
promise
prophet
quail
questions
quickly
rainbow
remember
replied
rest
rise
risen
river
rode
rotted

rough
ruled
ruler
Sabbath
safe
Samaritan
Samuel
Saul
Savior
scratches
seashore
seemed
sell
send
sending
sent
servant
setting
seventh
several
share
shared
sharing
sheepfold
shepherds
shone
shook
shut
sick
sickness
Siloam
Simeon
Simon Peter
sin
sinful
sixth

skin
skip
skipping
slave
slice
slingshot
soft
soldiers
son
spat
spear
special
Spirit
spoke
spread
stable
stood
strange
stretched
strong
stronger
students
stunned
such
sunshine
sword
sycamore
taken
taught
taxes
teaching
temple
third
though
threw
through

throw
thrown
tiny
tomb
touch
toward
trouble
true
trumpets
trusted
twelve
twice
twinkled
voice
waded
wake
warm
waved
wee
week
whole
whom
widow
wild
Wise-man
wore
worried
worry
worship
worshiped
wrote
yesterday
young
you're
Zacchaeus